By Alison DeNicola

10 9 8 7 6 5 4

Made in China

Published by
U.S. GAMES SYSTEMS, INC.
179 Ludlow Street
Stamford, CT 06902 USA
www.usgamesinc.com

Introduction

Divine Feather Messenger is inspired by my past and continuing personal experiences with feathers. The magical messages of feathers, the symbolism and connection to the bird kingdom and my great reverence and trust in the angelic realm have all encouraged me to bring these energies forward in an accessible and divinely guided way. This 44-card deck and book set unites the pure healing energies of the angelic realm with the earth-based symbolism of the bird kingdom. Each of the feather images chosen for this collection have been blessed and charged with the intention of messaging and healing for the user.

Many of us are familiar with the idea of "finding feathers" as an omen or sign of messaging. Often such an omen is noticed in connection to a world beyond. A beloved soul that has passed, a guardian angel's loving watch, a confirmation to a question that is on your mind are all times when feathers may be discovered. The bird kingdom, simply by its connection to the element of air and the sky, is the animal kingdom most closely related to the divine realm. Birds are not only seen as messengers of nature, they also appear as personal guides or totems for many spiritual teachers, masters and saints.

In addition, the bird and its feathers are among the oldest symbols of spirit, magic, and divinity in human culture. You may begin to notice that the appearance of certain birds and feathers in your life coincides perfectly with your readiness to receive their messages. Birds of prey in particular usually show up to invite you to see things from a higher point of view. These birds, which include eagles, hawks, condors and owls, have played special roles in mythology, history and shamanism. In many cultures, the meanings of feathers are associated with ascension and spiritual evolution to a higher plane. Eagle feathers were worn by Native American chiefs on their headdress to act as antennae, and symbolize their communication with Great Spirit. Celtic Druid priests wore robes adorned with feathers to assist their transition to the sky realms from the earth. Ancient Greek, Roman, Egyptian and Hindu gods and goddesses had birds as their symbolic companions and particularly feathers as their ascension tools. All of these traditions naturally blend the idea of the divine uniting with earth through the power of birds and feathers.

Of all of these different associations, the angelic realm is the most natural and reoccurring place for the symbols of feathers. We acknowledge the archangels who work as the angels in service to humanity. We often see angels and white feathers together as natural companions of blessing and healing.

Divine Feather Messenger deck seeks to unite the energies of heaven and earth. This is the natural alignment of universal themes. "As above, so below" is a powerful statement reminding us that we are connected to both realms and are being invited to deepen that connection.

—Alison DeNicola

"Once you have tasted flight, you will forever walk the earth with your eyes turned skyward, for there you have been, and there you will always long to return."

—Leonardo da Vinci

Note: The images of the birds and feathers are not shown to scale.

Working with the Divine Feather Messengers

Always begin with the following in mind:

- Be grateful. Feathers are a unique and pure symbol of nature and our connection to the natural world. Gratitude is a beautiful way to honor yourself and all that your life offers.

- Be open. Allow the messengers to inform you through their color, light and messages. Having the intention to believe and allow is essential. Notice how your relationship to spirit, inspiration and your life's path is deepened in this process.

- Be intuitive. Feathers are like a communication tool from a higher power. Use all of your senses to allow your own intuition to deepen. Listen to the messages and allow your unique perspective to shift and grow.

- Be love. Feathers often show up when there is someone or something that wants to reach out to us. Air is the element that represents the heart. Allow yourself to tap into your heart with a deeper reverence, connection and acceptance.

In this deck, you will find the first four cards to be the special "white" divine healers offering a unique viewpoint; the higher message and vision of divine healing. The remaining 40 cards represent the beautiful and varied energies of the birds chosen. As you come to know these guides, you will see that each has a specific message. They are all accompanied by information regarding their seasonal influence, elemental connection and color associations. Each card also presents keywords as well as an affirmation to work with.

As you will see, the Divine Feather Messengers represent many different aspects of inspiration and messaging. There are some generally acknowledged "keywords" associated with feathers as listed here:

Angels, Abundance, Spirit, Travel, Heaven,
Lightness, Flight, Messages, Ascension, Prayer

Divine Feather Messenger is a double-sided deck. The feather side represents the simple but powerful image of the feathers and is designed to be fanned out when preparing to select your messenger cards. The reverse side of the card holds the name of the bird, the beautiful watercolor image of the bird and an inspirational message.

The cards are meant to be used as an informative healing tool. Simply choose a card and tune into the divine messenger. Each feather card has been imprinted with the healing energy of the angels, so take time to notice the image and the message it offers. You can then receive more information by reading the detailed message in the book. Be aware of how it relates to a question you may have or it may be a general message that you might need right now. You can expand on the energies by using the affirmation provided.

A perfect way to do this is to begin a short meditation using the four principles outlined on page 6. Open your heart and ask for the divine message that is perfect for you today. Choose one card and work with the message for that day or a longer period of time. Repeat the affirmation as often as you feel called to do so.

You can also call on the Divine Feather Messengers as a part of your ongoing relationship with nature. Choose one or more cards and ask to work with these energies on a deeper level. Take this awareness out into nature wherever you are. Observe which elements, colors and seasonal connections resonate for you. Notice the birds, feathers and sky. You may discover that once you set your focus on the bird kingdom, feathers will start appearing with more frequency.

You may want to work with the cards in a traditional three-card spread. Come to stillness, shuffle and fan the cards, then choose three cards to represent past, present and future.

Messages for:

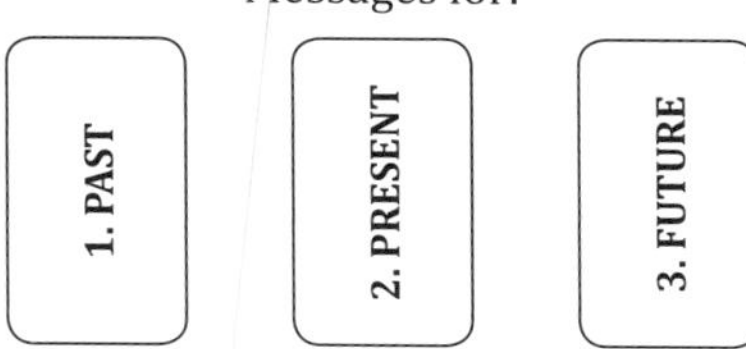

1. Where you are leaving
2. Where you are now
3. New energies emerging

Call on the divine healing grace of the angels and bird kingdom to guide you as you do.

Elements

The messages are followed by a notation of which elements are present within each bird energy. Each element has unique physical, emotional and mental qualities as outlined here:

Earth—Grounding, Stable, Practical, Abundant,

Physical, Safety, Family, Connected

Water—Flowing, Buoyant, Flexible, Fluid, Adaptable, Emotional, Playful, Creative

Fire—Energetic, Transformative, Confident, Warm, Courageous, Self-important, Lively

Air—Light, Moving, Sensitive, Open, Free, Cerebral, Loving, Compassionate, Flighty

We explore four elements to give more depth and connection to the natural world. (The fifth element known as space or ether element is not used here.)

Seasons

Each Divine Feather Messenger is connected to seasonal influence primarily tied into the bird and its migration pattern. Seasons have unique symbolism and may assist in uncovering further influences on your message.

Spring—New beginnings, Rebirth, Renewal, Growth

Summer—Light, Expression, Action, Vitality

Fall—Maturity, Harvest, Change, Reflection

Winter—Quiet, Introversion, Introspection, Contemplation

Each season offers us a different viewpoint into the bird kingdom.

Colors

Each of these colors has a unique quality that is so beautifully expressed in nature. Using color as a means for connecting to deeper meaning is a potent way to expand on the messages as well.

White: Purity, Healing, Divine innocence

Black: Protection, Mystery, Magic

Red: Vitality, Passion, Survival

Orange: Creativity, Joy, Emotions

Yellow: Cheer, Self-esteem, Brightness

Green: Love, Health, Compassion

Blue: Communication, Expression, Freedom

Grey: Balance, Neutrality, Softness

Brown: Earth, Richness, Stability

Purple: Intuitive, Magical, Rich

Cream: Calmness, Warmth, Relaxed

Gold: Prosperity, Wisdom, Knowledge

Divine Feather Messenger

Feather Messages

White Swan

Swans are mighty in size and power, yet soft with their effortless glide in motion. The swan has long been a symbol of beauty, grace, fidelity and partnership. The symbolism is enhanced by the color white; the color of healing, purity and the angelics. Swan is also a symbol for transformation. Many folktales use swan to illustrate the shift from the duckling or child self into the fullness of maturity. Goddesses have also chosen swan as their mount, like the divine goddess Saraswati, who unites with the healing element of water in her quest for wisdom, knowledge and the arts.

Message: The white swan brings with it the message that the power of divine grace is indeed with you and within you. Your connection to source is powerful and the healing potential is connected with your collected merits in the form of grace. Now is the time to embrace these divine gifts where you most need support. That healing may be in the form of a blessing over a current situation or transformation occurring in your life. Know that the divine messengers are assisting you now. You have the power through your own grace to move through any situation or challenge you are facing in a smooth and harmonious way.

Energies: Grace, Beauty, Fidelity, Transformation

Season: Summer

Element: Water, Air

Color: White (purity and healing)

Affirmation: I now accept the gift of divine grace and choose to honor the power and healing light within.

White Turkey

The turkey has long been a symbol of abundance, wisdom, earth and giving back. The symbolism is enhanced by the color white; the color of healing and purity. White turkey therefore is the symbol for healing the earth and our call to earth healing. The turkey in North America is most commonly a symbol of the harvest, the abundance of the season and a turkey that is sacrificed as the "give back" to feed the group. The white turkey is not so common and calls us to recognize the uniqueness of this symbol and the power of its message.

Message: The white turkey brings with it the

message that the earth is calling for healing now. Your connection to the earth and your need and desire to receive healing will be divinely guided. As you focus on earth healing—whether through environmentalism, blessing the land and water, or contributing to preservation efforts—you will assist in healing your own personal earth energies. These may be related to abundance, to your physical body, or to family issues. The white turkey comes to assist you as a mirror. As we heal the earth, we heal ourselves.

Energies: Earth-based healing, Abundance, Divine wisdom

Season: Fall

Element: Earth, Air

Color: White (purity and healing)

Affirmation: I am open to receive the divine abundance and healing of the earth.

White Eagle

Eagle is the bird totem associated with spirit and is often seen as divine guidance and vision. The white eagle has a special connection to the angelic realm as a messenger of the divine. White eagle calls us to our highest connection to source, to our soul's purpose and to our service here on earth. White eagle tail feathers are commonly used in the headdresses of Native American chiefs as the antennae to Great Spirit and that connection demands great responsibility. When we are in service for the highest good, it is a call to follow our soul's true path here on earth.

Message: The white eagle delivers the message that now is the time to come into alignment with your soul's unique purpose. We are all being called to awaken at this time and receive our divine inheritance. It is time to let go of fear, move ahead and step into the power of your soul. Whether you are called to service through healing work or service to humanity, see your unique energy and contribution as vital to the shift now taking place. Expand out from where you stand and see if you can use your gifts to assist and guide those around you.

Energies: Soul's purpose, Highest vision, Power

Season: Summer

Element: Fire, Air

Color: White (purity and healing)

Affirmation: I awaken to my soul's unique and divine purpose.

White Owl

The owl is a bird of mystery, omens and the gifts of the unseen. The white owl is a unique messenger who brings light into the shadows. The mystery of owl is suddenly illuminated by the light of the divine and calls us to our highest intuition, knowledge and awareness. Many of the ancient wisdom goddesses kept owl as their wise counsel. The white owl signifies the wisdom of divine guidance coming through. We first need to be ready, willing and able to listen to this guidance from spirit and then have the faith to follow it.

Message: The white owl awakens a keener sense of listening, seeing, sensing and knowing. This divine messenger encourages you to follow your intuition and allow those senses to expand as you do so. Our ability to connect to the divine messengers is a skill that needs to be used for the highest good. Now is the time to pay attention to the messages you are receiving whether through synchronicity, repetitive thought or direct revelation. Follow the guidance that asks only for the best and highest good for all.

Energies: Intuition, Wisdom, Knowing

Season: Fall

Element: Air

Color: White (purity and healing)

Affirmation: I honor the messages and guidance of the divine that arise within me.

Blackbird

The blackbird has long been considered a bird of mystery with its unique folklore. This is a messenger who often communicates through his loud and magical song. Blackbirds with their dark plumes are associated with the unseen worlds and are thought to be the gateway to unseen reality. Blackbirds remind us that not everything is as it seems to the naked eye.

Message: The blackbird calls you to the unseen realms. This messenger encourages you to welcome in the mysteries and magic of that which is not in plain sight. Allow the song of blackbird to invite you to move beyond your usual limits and find your hidden potential. The gifts that we find in the shadows are often the greatest inspirations. All we need to do is step forward and seek what is right there in the twilight. Allow yourself to push past the ordinary boundaries and take the journey with blackbird. As you do, be open to the new information and opportunities that await you.

Energies: Mystery, Hidden potential

Season: Spring, Summer, Fall

Element: Air, Water

Color: Black, Red

Affirmation: I embrace and open to the mystery and magic in life.

Bluebird

The bluebird is usually associated with the qualities of joy, peace, harmony and union. Bluebirds are often pictured in happy pairs, signifying fidelity and blissful partnerships. Many stories surround bluebird from native folklore to modern day tales. The color blue is significant in its beauty, its connection to the element of air and to the throat chakra. The bluebird asks us to examine our own sense of inner peace and self-love. The happiness we seek begins on the inside.

Message: The bluebird flies into your space to deliver the great blessings of peace, joy and happiness. This messenger reminds you to honor the purity of your speech and communication—especially those messages that you feed to yourself. The lightness and color of bluebird help make you aware of the spiritual links of the sky and the realms beyond. Invite the tranquility of bluebird into any area of your life that could use more lightness. Then, share the energy of bluebird with those around you. Have you forgotten the simple pleasures of life? Bluebird is here to remind you that it is okay to let go and fly for sheer pleasure. As you do, feel the weight of life lifted and soar higher up into the blue sky.

Energies: Happiness, Joy, Peace

Season: Winter, Spring

Element: Air

Color: Blue

Affirmation: I invite a deeper sense of peace and joy into my life.

Blue Jay

Blue jay has often been associated with the qualities of aggression and dominance in the bird kingdom, yet they are remarkably versatile birds. Their markings signify higher knowledge and they are adaptable, with incredible skills of survivorship and family bonding. Blue jays are often observed in family groups hunting and gathering together and defending their space. The jay is a noticeably talkative bird and the correlation between their vibrant blue coloring and the throat chakra points to communication and essential truths.

Message: The energy of blue jay invites you to step forward and uncover your mastery. What is in need of support to realize a goal? This messenger reminds you that there are many paths to one end. There are times when we need to access a variety of skills and behaviors—some more forceful and others more passive. True mastery lies in the integration of all of the qualities, skills and traits you possess and using them appropriately. Look at the parts of yourself you have disowned, disavowed or denied and then invite them to return. True mastery is found in wholeness and truth.

Energies: Mastery, Communication, Family

Season: All year round

Element: Earth, Air

Color: Blue, White, Black

Affirmation: I reclaim all parts of myself and open to my highest potential.

Canary

The canary is a songbird that is thought to have originally migrated from the Canary Islands. The canary has symbolic ties to musicianship and the power of sound and sound healing. They also have close associations with vocal and speech expressions. These birds also signify awakening and heightened sensitivity to the elements. The sensitive nature of canary reminds us to use our voice to uplift, inspire and heal rather than to disempower ourselves and others.

Message: The beautiful tones of your unique song are now coming together in a new way. Let go of hesitation and step fully into empowered expression. This may be a call to music, sound healing, speaking your truth or teaching others. Be aware that what you have to say and how you express it is important. What song are you singing to yourself? Allow canary to show you the way to bring your voice and expressions forward so that your song can be heard. Stepping into empowered expression is truly accelerated growth. Allow canary to guide you through.

Energies: Communication, Sensitivity

Season: All year round

Element: Fire, Air

Color: Yellow, Blue

Affirmation: I allow my expression to awaken. I am unique and valued.

Cardinal

Cardinal with its bright red plumage is seen year round but is most noticeable in the winter months. The males are decidedly more vibrant and showy, while the females are usually a more subtle shade of red. Cardinals have a distinctive call and they stay with their mates for life. This messenger has long been associated with important and essential qualities, such as the "cardinal directions" in the Native American medicine wheel. Some tribes call the cardinal "daughter of the sun," further linking this bird to the element of fire, vitality and enthusiasm.

Message: Examine the opportunities in your life where a path to leadership may be opening up for you. Moving forward requires self-awareness and confidence in your unique qualities and gifts. Feel assured of your importance on this journey. Cardinal is calling you to see yourself in a new light. Use that light to move forward while you lead others to do the same. Cardinal bestows a special message of self-worth. Choose to claim this as a right and a truth.

Energies: Leadership, Self-worth, Vitality, Confidence

Season: Winter

Element: Fire, Air

Color: Red, Black

Affirmation: I embrace and open to new opportunities with confidence.

Chickadee

Chickadee is a small but mighty bird that often serves as the community messenger. Their unique song is considered to bring "news" to others in their habitat. They have unusual brain patterning that allows them to shed old information each fall to create space for new information and to keep adapting to the changing environment. The chickadee messenger signals communication from others and encourages us to look at our own manner of expression. Is what we are saying truthful, supportive and kind? Chickadee urges us to review our patterns and see what needs to be released.

Message: Chickadee reminds us of the value of reviewing our lives to assess where there is room for letting go so that we may invite in the new. Clearly examine your communications—to others as well as yourself—to notice what patterns or habits may be weighing you down. Are you stuck in a rut? Are your dreams delivering messages? Chickadee chirps to remind you to pay attention to words, actions and signs of changes to come.

Energies: Communication, Activity, Adaptability

Season: Spring, Fall

Element: Earth, Air

Color: Black, White, Grey, Brown

Affirmation: I choose to surrender all thoughts, words and patterns that hold me back.

Condor

Condor is a type of vulture found in the high mountain regions of the American West and South America. Their wingspan is enormous, some around nine feet wide, which allows them to fly long distances high up in the air. Condor feathers are commonly used in shamanic healing, ceremonies and rituals. Condors are seen as the bird visionaries who have survived despite struggles. They show emotions through the changing color of their skin. They serve the environment as many vultures do by cleaning up and digesting the remains of other creatures. Condor is also associated with the sun and can symbolize illumination, power and spirituality.

Message: Condor flies high overhead and soars inward to urge you to see the broad vision of your life. Use the power of color in art or your surroundings to express your emotional nature, as condor does. If you have been engaged in a struggle or hardship, rest assured that you are now in possession of what it takes to move past it. There is no longer a barrier to your highest vision. Make sure that you take time to see exactly what that vision is and move toward it with the strength and stamina that has been revealed. Know that you are now exactly where you are meant to be.

Energies: Improvement, Power, Adaptability

Season: Winter, Fall

Element: Earth, Air

Color: Black, White, Grey, Brown

Affirmation: My highest vision is spacious. I embrace all that awaits me.

Crane

Crane is a uniquely shaped bird with a long beak and long legs. It is commonly associated with fidelity and marriage. In Asian cultures the crane is a messenger of longevity and healing, as the great bird is believed to have the ability to fly up to the heavens. The Zuni tribe regards the crane as the keeper of great secret magic. The crane's call is distinct and loud—warning those around them to watch out and pay attention. Crane is a water bird that will teach you to work with the element of water, which is feminine, emotional and adaptable.

Message: Crane sounds the call to empowering your relationships. The time is coming for forming a new partnership that will be supportive and long lasting. This union may be something you have been seeking or it may take you by surprise. Crane urges you to pay attention to those stepping forward into your life at this time. Be sure to use your emotional intelligence to see where you stand and what you are attracting. Is it for your highest good? If it is, take the leap of faith and go for it. You are in the right place to create a union that is perfect for you now.

Energies: Longevity, Creation, Union

Season: All year round

Element: Water, Air

Color: White, Grey

Affirmation: I am now ready to embrace and trust my divine partnerships.

Crow

Crow is a common bird that likes to test, intrigue and annoy. They can be found often in groups, creating sound in a "mob-like" fashion with their caw to warn or drive off predators. The common crow is black with dark blue or purple tones. It has deep associations with the nighttime, the maternal and the womb. Crows are highly intelligent sentinels who perch high in trees overseeing the flow of activity. They remind us that creation and magic are part of the cosmic energies. Under the guidance of universal laws, we find an incredible road map for manifesting our desires.

Message: The crow is a wise messenger of the power of creation. Crow speaks the language of the universal creator and asks you to go into the darkness to tap into your manifesting ability. Pay attention to messages, visions and signs. The universal laws govern all and tell us that there is an unending field of potential that can be accessed. You can think of it as magic or universal energy—it matters not. The energy of crow is urging you to start creating all that you desire. Crow playfully reminds you to enjoy the process.

Energies: Creation, Universal laws, Communication

Season: All year round

Element: Earth, Air

Color: Black, Purple

Affirmation: I acknowledge my own higher connection. I am a powerful channel.

Dove

The dove is a beautiful symbol of peace, motherhood and the qualities associated with the feminine. Dove has a long association with the goddess and other traditional mother symbols. In many cultures, a dove appears with an olive branch bringing a message of peace. Doves are monogamous and are often heard "cooing" with their partners at dawn and dusk—the times of day often thought of as portals to the spiritual world. The dove's cry is associated with the sound of mourning, reminding us to let go of what has passed while we open our hearts to the now.

Message: Dove delivers the message of peace, love and blessings. Now is the perfect time to open up to a deeper sense of tranquility and balance. Have you felt in harmony with the world and with your life? Are you holding onto anything that is keeping you from feeling at peace? Dove floats down to share the message that serenity lies within. Stop and take a breath. Connect to the energy and be open to receive. Once you come back to this place of inner peace you will feel a greater connection between your inner world and all that surrounds you. This is a blessing indeed.

Energies: Peace, Happiness, Serenity

Season: All year round

Element: Earth, Water, Air

Color: White, Ivory, Grey

Affirmation: Peace is within and all around me. I accept and share this with others.

Duck

There are many varieties of duck, almost all living on both land and water. The feminine quality of water is important to this bird as it links to the emotional body and to the general idea of nurturance and flow. In spite of their close connection to earth and water, most ducks can also fly, making them adaptable to their circumstances. Ducks are playful, affectionate and community oriented and will often return to where they feel safe and comfortable. Ducks remind us to look at how we are sailing our own seas and consider if we are placing ourselves in areas that support us best.

Message: Duck is the messenger who glides into your awareness now. If you have felt out of your element or without a safety net, the duck feather reminds you to come back to the people, places and surroundings that make you feel most at home. Very often, the busyness of life can take us off course. Our friendships and sense of community can help us to reconnect in a positive way. Duck's friendly message encourages you to revisit old friendships or find new connections that will give you a sense of ease and comfort. Remember to let go a bit so you can walk, float or fly when you need to. Duck weathers the emotional storms and lets go in this way too.

Energies: Emotional support, Comfort, Community

Season: Spring, Summer

Element: Earth, Water, Air

Color: White, Brown, Teal, Green, Black

Affirmation: I welcome friends and surroundings that offer support and safety.

Eagle

The eagle is a mystical symbol of the sun and sky, a messenger of spiritual knowledge. Eagle is also held as a representation of higher authority, heroic nobility and power. Many cultures honor eagle feathers as sacred ceremonial tools. Air is the main element of eagle, representing the realm of higher mind and inspiration. Eagles possess incredibly keen vision and are among the longest living birds—some living up to 25 years.

Message: As you begin to soar with eagle you are able to reach new levels of spiritual understanding, knowledge and connection. The eagle feather indicates that a great spiritual awakening is happening or that it is just on the horizon. The power and grace of eagle is a steady reminder that this call demands personal responsibility. As you begin to raise your vibration and perspective it is important to notice what you "see" from this higher place. Use this vantage point to bring new visioning into your life. Hold on as eagle takes you to your highest point yet. Know that the divine energy of Great Spirit watches over eagle as well as you.

Energies: Power, Perception, Spiritual insight, Knowledge

Season: Summer

Element: Fire, Air

Color: White, Black, Brown, Yellow

Affirmation: I am awakening now to my power, knowledge and vision.

Falcon

Closely tied to the Egyptian god Horus, who is known as possessing the all-seeing eye, falcon directs awareness to the third eye chakra or the place of seeing and vision. Vikings among others often used falcon and other birds of prey for hunting. This type of hunting and detection, commonly called falconry, was used in many ancient civilizations, tying this messenger to past lives. There are many types of falcons and they all have keen vision, great speed and amazing perception, allowing them to dive quickly and use their skills for fullest advantage.

Message: The falcon messenger has swooped in to show you that you indeed have the skills, perception and ability to attain the prize. What have you been seeking? Do you have a clear picture of your target? Whether this is an on-going quest or a new opportunity, you are being urged to hone your senses and take the leap without further delay. A sharp perception and an unwavering focus will assist you as you do. This may require you to move in a faster way than you might be accustomed to doing. Feel the power, skill and excitement of falcon supporting you as you take flight.

Energies: Power, Perception, Empowerment

Season: Summer, Fall

Element: Fire, Air

Color: White, Brown

Affirmation: I follow my instincts and achieve my highest goals.

Finch

Finch is a feather messenger who heralds the abundance of joyful opportunities. Native Americans referred to the finch as the "bird of happiness." They believed the bright yellow color of this bird was a gift from the gods that would bring bright joy, abundance and freedom into their lives. They also thought the song of the finch was the pure sound that announced the arrival of spring, which meant new opportunities and increased activity. Finch's many varied species remind us of the endless array of choices that life provides.

Message: This feather messenger has brought you the gift of abundance in the form of opportunity. Finch lands lightly as it is filled with the high vibration of new activity. Are you going too fast to see it? Are you managing your energy so that you will be ready when opportunity strikes? Balancing activity with rest can set the perfect stage for new openings to emerge. Remember that finch also reminds us through its lightness and connection to air to watch our mental activity in this way as well.

Energies: Vitality, Energy, Abundance

Season: Summer

Element: Air

Color: White, Brown, Red, Grey, Yellow

Affirmation: I am ready to embrace and welcome new abundance and light.

Flicker

A member of the woodpecker family, the flicker derives its name from the sound it makes. Because of their ability to make a variety of sounds, flickers are connected not only to drumming, but also to the mysteries of music and rhythm. This messenger connects you to the different rhythms in the world and especially to the heartbeat of the earth. This is the primal rhythm of life as we know it. The black and white coloring of flicker's markings is significant as well. It suggests the phases of the new moon, most often signifying the beginning of a new cycle.

Message: The divine flicker is the master drummer bringing awareness to what now is growing, moving and beating a new path in your life. This will be presented as a fluid and adaptable shift. Now is the time to examine your past patterns and experiences during these shifts. Do you resist following the natural rhythms of change? Self-limits are generally our most formidable hurdles. Use the great gifts of flicker to help you through any resistance. Trust that change is a sign of positive movement forward.

Energies: New rhythm, Growth

Season: Summer

Element: Earth, Air

Color: White, Black, Red

Affirmation: I trust in the infinite rhythms and flow of life.

Goose

Goose has long been represented in mythology, folklore and fairy tale stories signifying ideas, expression and the power of the quest. The goose that laid the golden egg is a classic storyline about seeking and fulfillment. The goose feather has long been used as a standard writing instrument and represents communication and creativity. The migration patterns of geese might inspire our own journey of fulfillment by expanding to other worlds and experiences.

Message: The goose messenger has arrived to

awaken you. All of those unfulfilled dreams and desires are stirring new energy within you and urging you to set out on a great quest. Now is the time to reflect on your deeper desires and what brings you a sense of joy. Then, with the great movement of goose, pursue it swiftly. Does it seem impossible? This is no longer the case. The journey awaits you with open arms.

Energies: Travel, Communication, Fulfillment

Season: Spring, Fall

Element: Earth, Water, Air

Color: White, Black, Grey, Brown

Affirmation: I now embark on my true quest and open my heart to fulfillment.

Grouse

Grouse is a large game bird that is closely linked to sacred dance and higher mind states. This feather messenger is a powerful symbol of the sacred spiral and the path inward. The Sufis use this form of whirling movement as a way to connect to higher levels of consciousness and higher guidance. Sacred dance has been a part of every society throughout the world. The dances very often represent the union of the divine masculine and feminine. This feather can signify our own need to integrate and balance masculine and feminine energies.

Message: Grouse spirals and whirls as the divine messenger of movement. Dance the sacred dance as an intention to reclaim and connect to your highest guidance. The dance can take the form of free-flow movement, yoga, kirtan or any other rhythmic practice that allows you to go into a meditative state. It is here, in this sacred place of stillness surrounded by movement, that we can connect more fully. A new flow of energy brought in by any inspired movement will support the process.

Energies: Movement, Stillness, Life cycle

Season: Spring

Element: Earth, Air

Color: White, Black, Brown

Affirmation: I seek and open to the unique sacred spiral within me.

Hawk

Hawk feather is a powerful messenger of communication as well as intuitive and visionary perception. This raptor is the messenger representing the light that illuminates darkness. In ancient Greece the hawk was sacred to the sun god Apollo, and likewise in Egypt, to the sun god Ra. Its connection to the sun further suggests hawk's amazing ability to "see" truths. Their nests are often high in the top of the tallest trees and their flight overhead can signify a confirmation of your intuitive perceptions. These divine messengers tend to arrive at the perfect moment, especially when you need direction concerning your path in life.

Message: Hawk has flown in to deliver a special message to you today. The energy of hawk confirms what you may already know or it opens your spiritual perception so that you may receive the message. Tune into this divinely guided communicator to see where you might receive more insight or information. Hawk directs you to see what you might have been missing. If you have been ignoring your own intuition or the synchronicities around you, it is time to listen and become aware now.

Energies: Communication, Vision, Messages

Season: Spring, Fall

Element: Air

Color: White, Black, Brown

Affirmation: Insight and inspiration are my divine messengers. I listen and accept their guidance.

Heron

There are several variations of heron, all of which are waders. The connection to the shallow waters implies the strong influence of the water element, reflection and the realm of emotions. Herons are often observed walking their own solitary path, symbolizing the attributes of self-reliance and self-support. Their enormous wingspan and powerful flight captures attention and highlights their beautiful and unique presence in the world. Herons embody the quality of patience and are said to represent the resolution of conflicts between other birds.

Message: The heron messenger wades into your world to encourage you to embrace your unique path. Let go of the pressure to conform to unwritten rules that may be keeping you stuck. As you begin to steady yourself and find a different way around an old and familiar pattern, you will feel more certain that you can indeed stand on your own in this way. Your unique viewpoint can assist others in resolving issues and can help bring harmony. The power of heron urges you to look into your surrounding world and reflect with a patient and loving heart. Let go of judgments and allow your personal path to unfold.

Energies: Self-reliance, Balance, Choice

Season: Spring

Element: Water, Air

Color: White, Blue, Grey, Brown

Affirmation: I now embrace and accept my true life's purpose.

Hummingbird

A passionate lover of freedom, the delightful hummingbird embodies beauty, lightness and joy. Hummingbirds can fly backwards and can hover in one place in the air. These attributes represent a re-awakening of the past and an ability to stay in the present moment. Hummingbird is also associated with nectar, the sweetness of life, and was very often called upon in Native American rain prayers. Hummingbird is tiny but its message is great.

Message: The hummingbird messenger signals

the time of new joy and accomplishments in your life. It is important to let go of any burdens or negativity so that you may fully receive the gifts on their way. Past desires, dreams and new opportunities are surfacing. Hummingbird signals the time is right to embrace all of these blessings. Slow down, take time to enjoy the process and sip the sweetness of this upcoming period. Lightness of being is the gift of hummingbird.

Energies: Joy, Sweetness, Freedom

Season: Summer

Element: Air

Color: Red, White, Green

Affirmation: I am light, joyful and free. I embrace the sweetness of life.

Kingfisher

There are many myths and legends about the ancient origins of the intriguing kingfisher. One tale indicates that kingfisher was the first bird Noah released from the ark after the flood. Flying high to the edge of the sun the kingfisher absorbed the blue color of the sky. From this story, the kingfisher has come to be associated with the promise of new warmth and abundance. Kingfisher feathers were carried in the old world as good luck charms. Kingfisher is a bold bird that fishes for its food, drawing new opportunities out of the waters. Connecting with the energy of this bird supports the manifestation of new abundance.

Message: Kingfisher messenger dives into your awareness with the promise of abundance and prosperity. Urging you to have faith and take the plunge, this divine messenger is a reminder that prosperity comes in many forms. New love, warmth and opportunities are among the favored gifts. This feather messenger also indicates that luck is with you. Stop trying so hard to create; just allow the natural flow of abundance to come to you. Prepare by being open to receive. The gifts of prosperity are now assured.

Energies: Prosperity, Luck, New warmth

Season: Summer

Element: Air, Water

Color: Red, White, Green, Grey, Blue

Affirmation: My world is loving and abundant. I open to receive these gifts.

Loon

Loon is a rather large water bird with tremendous swimming abilities. Mostly associated with the water element, loon sounds its haunting and primal cry during the in-between times of the day. Its call—sometimes sounding like a laugh, at other times a howl—is regarded as a true call of the wild. Many myths and stories describe the loon's cry as a wake-up call to a new state of consciousness. There are also tales connecting the loon to the faerie world, dream realms and astral travel.

Message: This feather messenger urges you to pay attention to your dreams. Dreams are the extension of the unseen worlds, whether from our subconscious mind or from the many realms beyond this physical world. With the presence of the loon, your dreams may seem more colorful and filled with more symbolism and messages. Keep a dream journal to record what you experience. Your dreams may be calling your attention to certain situations or giving you valuable input. Now is the time to listen and be aware.

Energies: Dreams, Messages, Consciousness

Season: Summer

Element: Air, Water

Color: Black, White

Affirmation: My dreams and visions are powerful, vibrant and clear.

Magpie

Magpie is a messenger associated in folklore with great luck and fortune. These highly intelligent birds are also extremely social. The magpie takes much time carefully building its nest with great attention to detail. Magpie is legendary for its attraction to shiny things, which it collects and hoards. Thus, the bird is associated with a tendency for materialism or valuing things for their appearance. The magpie feather is a reminder that the world we live in tends to be obsessed with materialism too. The black and white of magpie shows us how important it is to find balance in the duality of our earthly and spiritual paths.

Message: Magpie is reminding you that any obsession with material things or achievements will not nurture your spiritual path. The latest and greatest home, car or gadget will not help you get any closer to true contentment. Now is a good time to re-evaluate where you are and notice if you have become distracted by the accumulation of physical things. This messenger also brings the promise of good luck by way of magical opportunity. Finding a balance between the inner and outer worlds is the message of magpie.

Energies: Materialism, Balance, Good fortune

Season: Spring, Summer

Element: Air

Color: Black, White

Affirmation: I seek only what is needed to stay balanced and true to my path.

Meadowlark

The meadowlark messenger is in its true essence cheerful. Its bright yellow breast is the color of sunshine, positivity and a cheery disposition. It also marks the solar plexus chakra. The inner journey is one to the self and the discovery of deeper awareness, intuition and innate abilities. Because it sings while it flies, unlike most birds that sing from their perch, the meadowlark is associated with playfulness and a lighthearted nature.

Message: Meadowlark pops in to share the good news. You are in for a wonderful adventure of self-discovery. This experience may be connected to your spiritual path, your intuition or a greater sense of self-knowing. It can also be an unfolding of inner creativity and new projects. What is it that makes you smile? Are you ready for the next phase of your development? Meadowlark shows you that this growth comes from a place of inner strength, confidence and wonder. Use your sense of playfulness, too, in this discovery. It will help you to sing and fly at the same time.

Energies: Self-development, Cheerfulness

Season: Summer

Element: Earth, Air

Color: Black, Yellow, White

Affirmation: I choose to treasure the welcome gift of my own inner light.

Nuthatch

Nuthatch is a small bird with interesting and unique qualities. When he flies, he is up among the treetops. When he walks along the branches and trunks he does so in a zigzag motion with his head facing downward. The nuthatch gets its name from its habit of storing seeds and nuts in small spaces for later use. This practical quality urges us to take stock and plan ahead accordingly. The white chest of the nuthatch symbolizes the purity of the heart. This tiny songbird encourages you to have faith in yourself and your higher wisdom.

Message: This divine messenger urges you to soar as high as you dare. Just be prepared to bring all of that energy, inspiration and insight back down to earth. All of the knowledge sought should be put into practical action. Have faith in your ability to do this. Nuthatch messenger also inspires us to take a different view, turning away from our usual way of doing things. Bringing a fresh outlook to an old situation, or simply seeing the world from the top down can be a welcome change. Your willingness to adapt is key in this process. Take the turn now and uncover the gifts and understanding that await you.

Energies: Grounding, Faith, New perspectives

Season: Summer

Element: Earth, Air

Color: Black, Blue, White, Grey, Brown

Affirmation: With unwavering faith, I allow a new viewpoint to emerge.

Oriole

Oriole is a vibrantly colored songbird that appears to harken the first days of summer. The feathers are orange and black, reflecting a bright energy or sunshine quality associated with the longer, warmer days. Association with the sun symbolically represents happiness, light, success, positive energy and new experiences. Oriole is also a weaver, creating a nest from plant fibers that is often hanging from forked branches. This messenger is thought to use its weaving skill to suspend time and travel through new doorways. This feather is symbolic of creative pursuits, new adventures and projects. Orioles are always positive harbingers of what is new and positive coming into the light.

Message: Oriole messenger alerts you that positive change is coming your way. You are being urged to embrace your connection to creativity and use it while you see opportunities ahead. This does not mean to focus solely on artistic output but also to employ creativity in all aspects of your life. Weave new ideas and innovative thinking into any venture. The sun is shining upon you ensuring success, happiness and a positive outcome. This messenger also reminds you to pause and see pleasure in the simple things. Is your tendency to see the obstacles? Move past that now and see the bright path laid out before you.

Energies: Happiness, New projects, Creativity

Season: Summer

Element: Air, Fire

Color: Orange, Yellow, Black

Affirmation: My creativity and projects are blessed with golden light.

Osprey

This sea bird is one of the largest birds of prey in North America. Ospreys are great providers, unfussy and very social. They build sturdy nests high up on top of poles or in tall trees near the sea. Known to migrate long distances, they come back over and over again to the same places to nest and nurture their young. Their skill and acute vision allows them to dive from the sky into the sea and catch their food effortlessly. This fishing skill allows them to be abundant and successful providers for their families. Thus, finding an osprey feather is a favorable omen for success, abundance and family life.

Message: Osprey swoops in and delights you with the message of success and abundance. This divine messenger encourages us to use our unique skills to provide what is needed and share it with others. It shows us that there is abundance available right now in the perfect form. Be sure to make your priorities clear and set your sights because now is the time to jump into something feet first. Osprey supports your success and encourages you to nurture yourself and to serve your family as well. Keep an open mind as you do, for it is certain that your view of abundance may shift and evolve.

Energies: Abundance, Success, Skill

Season: Summer, Fall

Element: Water, Air

Color: Black, White, Grey, Brown

Affirmation: I am grateful for the divine abundance in my life.

Ostrich

While he cannot fly, the ostrich is a creature of great strength and speed. This exotic bird with his head held high is seen as symbolizing higher knowledge and intuition. At the same time, he embodies grounding and a tangible connection to the earth. In mythology, the great Egyptian goddess Ma'at uses her feather of truth—the ostrich feather—to weigh the hearts of those passing at the end of life. If the heart is pure and good, the heart is sent with the soul to the upper world. If the heart is dark and impure, it is swallowed and dissolved. In this way, the feather of Ma'at represents justice served, based on right action and choice. While we seek higher knowledge, we should choose to use it in a practical and grounded way.

Message: Ostrich messenger invites you to reflect on your personal journey now. Have you been on an endless search for knowledge, teaching and wisdom? Maybe you have not yet begun. In either case, this divine messenger urges you to begin to move ideas and energy out of the mental realm and start to apply this information in a practical way. Using new knowledge is the way to move forward in life. Always remember to reflect on the truth of what you are "walking" in the world. Choose to lower your head occasionally like ostrich, not to bury it, but to look deeply inward. Honor what is true and just in your own heart.

Energies: Grounding, Truth, Choice

Season: All year round

Element: Earth

Color: Black, White, Grey, Brown

Affirmation: Truth guides my journey forward. I am fully grounded in this way.

Owl

A bird of the night, the owl has incredible vision and hearing. Owls hunt by using their listening skills, inviting us to tap into a greater sense of inner listening and awareness. The ancient goddess Athena carries an owl on her shoulder as a knowing companion who represents the wise counsel of nature. It was believed in ancient Rome that the owl feather placed on a sleeping person would reveal their deepest secrets. The owl is also a powerful symbol of the feminine and the moon and is often tied to prophecy and darkness. As a nocturnal bird, their appearance at dawn or dusk can be associated with the in-between times when the veil between the realms is the thinnest. In all these ways, owl is a powerful symbol of our own intuitive senses and abilities.

Message: Now is the time to start seeing things using the higher senses. Owl messenger is here to assure you that your intuition is correct. The darkness or murkiness that surrounds a certain situation is merely a perception. Begin to access your intuitive skills to see the answers clearly. It may be an inner sense of knowing, viewing, listening, or feeling that needs to be used separately or together. Have you been resisting listening to your inner wisdom? Owl messenger urges you to do so now. Allow there to be light within the darkness and find the answers you seek. Embrace this part of yourself as you do.

Energies: Intuition, Listening, Awareness

Season: Fall

Element: Air

Color: Black, White, Grey, Brown

Affirmation: My intuition is powerful and vibrant. I honor this inner wisdom.

Parrot

The parrot is brightly feathered and exotic, showing us its connection and importance to color and individuality. This messenger is also regarded as a bird of the sun and symbolizes the power of light. Parrots are often admired for their rich plumage, as well as their amazing ability to mimic what they hear. They can be trained to communicate through repetition. With this gift of being able to imitate humans, they are seen as a link between the bird kingdom and the human realm. We might see them as envoys but are reminded that they have been programmed to speak the thoughts and beliefs of others.

Message: The divine parrot messenger comes into your life to remind you to honor your unique voice. Very often we can get caught up in the judgments, opinions and values assigned to us by others. These are false truths. Your individuality and personal expression are being encouraged to come into the light. This may feel challenging, as it is safer and easier to hide in the shadows. Begin by paying attention to your own mind. Then, gently allow yourself to see all of your positive attributes, your personal colors and talents. It takes practice and courage to step out and embrace who you are. Parrot encourages you to do just that. Once you do, you will feel your truth easily coming to light.

Energies: Personal expression, Color, Individuality

Season: All year round

Element: Air

Color: Blue, Green, Yellow, Red, White

Affirmation: I honor my individuality and unique expression in the world.

Peacock

Many cultures, myths and traditions honor peacock, especially through the eye feathers, as a mystical and wise messenger of power and resurrection. In ancient Egypt, the peacock feathers were thought to be akin to the eye of Horus, the all-seeing watcher. The ancient Greeks honored peacock as the watchman over the goddess Hera. Peacock is the national bird of India and is represented through that culture's art in color, pattern and symbol. The peacock is closely associated with the phoenix rising from the ashes. Because of its enduring brilliance, the peacock feather came to symbolize resurrection in early Christianity.

Message: This wise messenger fans open to remind you that you are a soul first and foremost. The soul has a wisdom contained from every lifetime. Although you may not be aware of your inner wisdom, you are being awakened now to the wise, watchful soul that you possess. This may come in the form of a new outlook, renewed interests, reawakened learning or a more powerful process of shedding the old, worn out experiences in your life. As this process unfolds, know that you are on steady ground and be open to a rebirth in some area of your life. Trust that your wise soul is guiding you through your human experience. Holding the highest vision for yourself is the gift of this messenger. Finding the wisdom of your soul's long journey home is divine.

Energies: Vision, Rebirth, Watchfulness

Season: Spring, Fall

Element: Earth, Air

Color: Blue, Green, Gold, Brown

Affirmation: I invite a greater understanding of my soul's divine wisdom.

Pelican

The pelican is a water bird with an unmistakable pouch and bill. The bird is quite light and buoyant in spite of its size and is a symbol of lightness on the water. This imagery calls our attention to our own ability to rise above the heaviness of life. The water is a symbol of emotions and pelican teaches us to not become overwhelmed by them. Most importantly, pelican dives deep into the watery world of emotion and rises back up, urging us to do the same. The action of moving through the emotional world calls for selflessness and forgiveness. The weight of grudges, resentment and guilt can pull us down below the surface.

Message: Pelican messenger is here to share the power of forgiveness. Now is the time to take a look around your life and see what and who needs forgiveness and release. By attaching ourselves to old pain, judgment and resentments we cannot move forward. Forgiveness does not mean giving approval to others' behaviors or actions. The power of forgiveness is simply a gift to ourselves that allows us to let go of the past and feel lighter in the present. To forgive others can sometimes be easier than forgiving ourselves, so show yourself the grace of forgiveness. Let go of the weight of old guilt; forgive and rise above the surface of your life.

Energies: Forgiveness, Selflessness, Emotions

Season: Spring, Summer, Fall

Element: Water, Air

Color: Brown, White

Affirmation: I forgive everything and everyone, especially myself.

Pheasant

The modern pheasant is a larger bird that dwells in the hedges, brush and grassy areas. First traced back to an area in Greece near the Phasis River from which they derive their name, they are now considered a domesticated bird. For this reason, they have a symbolic association with family life and fertility. Their long tail feathers, commonly called plumes, are associated with sexuality, fertility, creativity and the expression of this energy. Pheasant feathers are varied in stripes, tapering and size and are generally warm in coloration. These traits are also associated with feathering the nest or creating a vibrant, comfortable home life.

Message: This divine messenger strolls in to share the gifts of renewed creativity and fertility in all aspects. Have you lost interest in a satisfying and fertile home life? With its warm colors and beautiful plumes, pheasant reminds us how important it is to have a place that feels harmonious and supportive. Not only do these energies enhance deeper connections with a partner, but they also provide fertile ground for creativity. Sexual energy is the creative force that manifests in many ways. It can generate new life in physical form or fuel creativity in projects and ideas. This may be an area you've neglected while busy working on other aspects in your life. Now is the time to stop and direct attention to your methods of connecting and creating.

Energies: Creativity, Fertility, Sexuality

Season: All year round

Element: Earth, Air

Color: Brown, White, Cream

Affirmation: I am vibrant, vital, creative and alive.

Raven

Raven is a symbolic messenger from the family of blackbirds. All of the blackbirds hold some level of mystery and magical energy. Raven is a power bird, decidedly aligned with the strong feminine energy of the universe. Often called a messenger of prophecy, raven calls us to tune in and take notice of what is happening around us. Odin of Norse mythology had two raven companions representing thought and memory. Recognizing the raven's sharp mind and keen intelligence encourages us to trust ourselves and our own supreme knowing.

Message: Raven's message is one of empowerment. His distinct caw awakens you to notice your personal power and to accept this as your truth. Oftentimes we ignore the signs on the path and deny our own importance. That time is officially over. You are being called to notice and follow the signs and synchronicities of the universe that will awaken your inner wisdom. You may feel called to a higher vision and reach for yourself. The blackness of the raven's feather represents untapped potential and the expansive universe. Follow the guidance of raven and own your power now.

Energies: Insight, Prophecy, Power

Season: Fall, Winter

Element: Earth, Air

Color: Black, Blue, Purple

Affirmation: I claim my divine power and open to unlimited potential.

Robin

The appearance of robin is traditionally seen as the symbol of spring. The season of new growth and emerging life is a positive one, as is the robin itself. Connecting all the way back to the time of ancient Norse myth and European lore, this messenger is seen as a symbol of good fortune. An awakening of new growth in all areas of life is associated with the robin's red breast. This color is symbolic of the activation of the root center and kundalini energy. Robin's beautiful blue egg is said to represent creativity and of course, new birth. Their song is cheery and helps to establish their harmonious territory in the world. Robin is not solely a symbol of spring; it also relates to the Yule and signifies brightness on the darkest days.

Message: This divine messenger lands to let

you know that new growth is right around the corner. Robin brings with it the positive and affirming message to open to new opportunities and expand outward. Allow yourself to see those opportunities in the form of a new project, business, job or relationship. You may have felt stagnant in one or more of these areas. Feel the flow of change begin. Robin also encourages you to step outside now and find the divine messages of nature—positivity, potential and growth—all offered in perfect form. Remember the seasons also represent change and you should begin to honor each cycle as a time of change in your life. Feel the blessing of robin as you do.

Energies: New growth, Good fortune, Cheer

Season: Winter, Spring

Element: Fire, Air

Color: Brown, Red

Affirmation: Each new opportunity is a gift and a blessing.

Starling

Starling is a bird that is at ease in both urban and rural areas. This messenger often travels and nests in immense flocks. They are generally talkative birds that have the ability to mimic sounds in their environments and incorporate them into their calls. Their chatter is indicative of a group mind and group behavior. The symbolism of starling is closely tied to the power of community. The yellow beak in springtime represents energy around the solar plexus chakra, and the perception of societal roles and self-esteem. The beak is also associated with having clear communication within the group.

Message: The starling messenger flies and flocks to inspire your social side. Stepping out into the world is the perfect remedy for spending too much time alone or in your head. The energy of group mind is powerful and can be a welcome change. It may be the time to re-evaluate your community ties and find the perfect place to land. Have you been too social, too dependent on the company of others? Create a smaller, more intimate way to connect so that you may receive the gifts of community without draining your energy. In all of these circumstances, you are being guided to notice the unique gifts that come through the power of the group. Use your clear communication to connect more deeply and authentically.

Energies: Community, Group mind,

Communication

Season: Spring

Element: Air

Color: Black, Yellow, White

Affirmation: I welcome others into my world and receive the gift of community.

Turkey

Turkey messenger is most often associated with the gifts of mother earth. Frequently called the 'earth eagle,' turkey is a large bird that can in fact fly. They have a long history and association with spirituality, custom and ritual. Turkey is symbolic in the U.S. as the offering on Thanksgiving. We express gratitude for the sacrifice of turkey and honor our time of harvest. Turkey feathers have an important place in the mythology of Native Americans and are honored as a symbol of wisdom.

Message: Turkey struts in to remind you to acknowledge your bounty and share it with others. The way forward is to use the power of gratitude, sharing and service to expand and raise your vibration. This messenger represents the bountiful cycles of mother earth. Have you forgotten just how blessed you are? See all that you possess—whether it is material plentitude or abundance on other levels, and make a commitment to share this wealth. You might do this through volunteering, donating, recycling or actively creating something to benefit others. You will find that you will grow richer in all ways through this process.

Energies: Abundance, Gratitude, Service

Season: Fall

Element: Earth

Color: Black, Brown, Red

Affirmation: I now choose to offer and share my bounty with others.

Vulture

The vulture is a powerful and large raptor that relies on others to kill prey and on their own incredible sense of smell to locate food. Its role as scavenger is highly necessary and valued. They possess a unique digestive system that allows them to purify the waste, which helps keep the environment in balance. Symbolically, they appear in ancient Greek and Pueblo traditions as a guardian of the mysteries of life and death. Their feathers are used in rituals for grounding and to symbolize the divine union of heaven and earth.

Message: Death of the old way is imminent. This is not a physical death but the letting go of outworn roles, thoughts and beliefs. The divine vulture messenger urges you to release the past and all that you have been holding onto. This process can be a struggle if you resist, or you could be filled with the ease of acceptance. The choice is up to you. Once you begin to move fully into this process, you open the doorway to a beautiful opportunity for rebirth and renewal. Vulture assures you through this process of purification that you will indeed have a fresh start. Allow this messenger to process what you let go of and recycle the energy. Allow yourself to reabsorb this energy and experience the renewal that follows.

Energies: Death, Purification, Rebirth

Season: Fall, Winter

Element: Earth, Air

Color: Black, Brown

Affirmation: I honor and accept all of my life experiences.

Woodpecker

Woodpecker is an intriguing bird with the ability to use its beak to bore into wood to extract insects. The woodpecker's brain is packed tightly inside of the skull to protect it from repeated impact. This pecking is their call, sometimes called the drumbeat, in lieu of song. The connection to drumming is mystical as well as shamanic. The drumbeat is called the heartbeat of mother earth and can symbolize new rhythms and paths opening. The coloring of woodpecker is black and white, sometimes with a red cap. The red reflects the awakening of new mental energies and the power of the mind.

Message: The divine woodpecker drums its way into your consciousness to suggest you use the power of discernment now. Using your mental energy and the fortitude you already possess will be essential in the path to realizing your goals. Notice if you tend to be hardheaded or stubborn in relation to what may be a challenge. Can you allow a new rhythm to come into your way of doing things? These are all the questions that woodpecker presents. Use the focus and fortitude of this messenger to hammer away in a purposeful way. As you find that the power to realize your dreams are supported by the universe, it will become easier to find the rhythm you seek.

Energies: Discernment, Fortitude, Wisdom

Season: Summer, Fall

Element: Earth, Air

Color: Black, White, Red

Affirmation: I align thought, wisdom and fortitude in all of my actions.

Wren

Wren is a small, springtime bird that is said to be the king of birds and lucky as well. Adored as much as the robin in lore, we see wren in many folktales as an adaptable and resourceful bird. His powerful voice gives the impression of a much larger bird and allowed it to sing all day with great confidence. The wren's sensitivity to temperature indicates that we too need to be sensitive to extremes. Wren is clever and the pagan traditions associated this messenger to the earth gods and goddesses with sharing their earth-based wisdom. The wrens help us to realize we are the sum of all of our gifts.

Message: The divine wren flutters in to remind

you that you already possess all the resources you need. Rather than seeking more, looking here and there, now is the time to stand strongly and confidently. In this acceptance of what is already present, you will create the shift you seek. Watch out for any tendency toward extreme behavior. It is important to find the balance rather than to overdo it. Being bold and confident comes from strength within, not from a false sense of self. Wren guides you beautifully through this new exploration and invitation to grow. The gift of this messenger is adaptability.

Energies: Confidence, Resources, Adaptability

Season: Winter, Spring

Element: Earth, Air

Color: Brown, Grey

Affirmation: My confidence and inner strength guide me forward.

About the Author

Alison DeNicola is a yoga and meditation teacher, energy healer and author living in Stamford, Connecticut. In addition, Alison is a certified hypnotherapist, IET Master Instructor and intuitive light worker who has studied and taught with amazing teachers far and wide. Her passion is to bring the energy of peace, self-healing and connection to all of those she meets using nature themes, angelic wisdom, meditation practices and yoga philosophy.

Alison is also the author of *Mudras for Awakening the Energy Body; Mudras for Awakening the Five Elements; Yoga Dogs Deck and Book set; Yoga Cats Deck and Book Set.*

Website: www.alisondenicola.com
Instagram: @alisondenicola
Facebook: Alison DeNicola

About the Artist

David Scheirer is a painter and illustrator specializing in watercolors. During his career he's had the pleasure of collaborating with various wildlife organizations including Audubon's Project Puffin in Maine and International Bird Rescue. He lives in Aberdeen, Maryland and is inspired by the nature and wildlife of the nearby Chesapeake Bay and East Coast.

Website: www.dswatercolors.com
Instagram: @dswatercolors
Facebook: facebook.com/dswatercolors/

Notes

Notes

For our complete line of tarot decks, books, meditation cards, oracle sets, and other inspirational products please visit our website:
www.usgamesinc.com

Follow us on    

Published by
U.S. GAMES SYSTEMS, INC.
179 Ludlow Street
Stamford, CT 06902 USA
www.usgamesinc.com